Let's pretend we are...
At Home

Karen Bryant-Mole

Heinemann
LIBRARY

First published in Great Britain by Heinemann Library, Halley Court, Jordan Hill, Oxford OX2 8EJ,
a division of Reed Educational & Professional Publishing Ltd.

OXFORD FLORENCE PRAGUE MADRID ATHENS MELBOURNE AUCKLAND KUALA LUMPUR
SINGAPORE TOKYO IBADAN NAIROBI KAMPALA JOHANNESBURG GABORONE
PORTSMOUTH NH (USA) CHICAGO MEXICO CITY SAO PAULO

Designed by Jean Wheeler

Commissioned photography by Zul Mukhida

Produced by Colourpath Ltd., Soho.

Printed and bound in Italy by L.E.G.O.

02 01 00 99 98
10 9 8 7 6 5 4 3 2 1

ISBN 0 431 04655 7

This title is also available in a hardback library edition (ISBN 0 431 04654 9).

British Library Cataloguing in Publication Data
Bryant-Mole, Karen
Let's pretend we are at home
1.Home economics - Juvenile literature
2.Readers (Primary)
I.Title II.At home
640

Words that appear in the text **in bold** can be found in the glossary.

Acknowledgements
The Publishers would like to thank the following for permission to reproduce photographs.
Chapel Studios; 7 and 15 Zul Mukhida, Positive Images; 5, Tony Stone Images; 9 Lawrence Migdale,
13 Laurence Monneret, 23 Dan Bosler, Zefa; 11, 17, 19, 21.

Every effort has been made to contact copyright holders of any material reproduced in this book.
Any omissions will be rectified in subsequent printings if notice is given to the Publisher.

Contents

Shopping

Aliyu is pretending that he has been shopping. He is carrying the shopping home in a basket.

This woman brought her shopping
home in the car.
A week's shopping for a hungry family
is far too heavy to carry.

Cooking

Asia is pretending to cook some food.
She made her cooker from a cardboard box.

This man is cooking some soup.
Real cookers get very hot.
Never play with a real cooker.

Meal times

Bartie is pretending to have a meal with his toys. They each have a knife, fork and spoon.

These people are using chopsticks to eat their meal. They pick up the food by holding it between the two chopsticks.

Washing up

Aliyu is washing up his toy tea-set.
He has a washing-up bowl, filled with warm, soapy water.

This woman uses a dishwasher to clean her dishes. She puts everything in and lets the machine do all the work.

Baby's bedtime

Alysha is getting her doll
ready for bed.
She is pretending to wash
the doll's face.

This baby is having a bath before he goes to bed.
He doesn't look very sleepy yet!

Housework

Homes can get very dusty. Edward is using a toy broom to sweep the floor.

This woman is vacuuming her floor.
The dust is sucked up inside the machine.

Gardening

Asia has a set of toy garden tools.
She is pretending to **rake** up leaves.

Garden tools are very useful.
This man is using a **lawn mower** to
cut the grass.
It does the work quickly and easily.

Working

Melissa is pretending to work from home. She has set up an office with a play telephone and toy computer.

People who work from home use telephones, computers and **fax machines** to keep in touch with other people.

Baking

William is using a small **rolling pin** to roll out some **play dough**. He has some plastic cutters which will cut out interesting shapes.

These children are helping to make
an apple pie.
The **pastry** has been rolled and cut
out to fit the pie dish

Washing the car

Melissa's toy car has
got all muddy.
She is using a damp
cloth to clean it.

This boy is washing the car with a sponge.
His father is using clean water to rinse it.

Glossary

fax machines machines that can send and print words and pictures

lawn mower a machine that is used to cut grass

pastry a mixture of flour, fat and water that is used to make pies

play dough a mixture that be rolled out, squashed, twisted and squeezed

rake collect up with a tool called a lawn rake

rolling pin a roller with a handle at each end

Index